BRITAIN IN OLD PHOTOGRAPHS

NOTTINGHAM
YESTERDAY AND TODAY

GEOFFREY O

Nottinghamshire County Council
Leisure Services

ALAN SUTTON PUBLISHING LIMITED

Alan Sutton Publishing Limited
Phoenix Mill · Far Thrupp · Stroud
Gloucestershire · GL5 2BU

First published 1995 in collaboration with
Nottinghamshire County Council, Leisure
Services Department

Cover photographs: (front) Castle Road,
c. 1955; (back) Lower Parliament Street, 1964.

British Library Cataloguing in Publication Data.
A catalogue record for this book is available from
the British Library.

ISBN 0-7509-0981-1

Typeset in 9/10 Sabon.
Typesetting and origination by
Alan Sutton Publishing Limited.
Printed in Great Britain by
Ebenezer Baylis, Worcester.

Upper Parliament Street, 1962.

Contents

High Pavement, 1960s. The trees stood at the front of High Pavement Unitarian Church. The buildings at the end of the street were on Weekday Cross and the rear of other properties on Drury Hill can be seen.

Introduction

In my previous book of old photographs, *The Changing Face of Nottingham*, I explained how I came to have taken a number of black and white photographs of various parts of the city. These were all of places which I knew were about to change because existing buildings were about to be demolished. The favourable reception which that book received led me to consider compiling a similar book from the remaining photographs. However, I realized that although I had more than enough pictures for another book, some would have been of the same scenes as those in the earlier book. I still had a smaller number of different pictures, but not enough to justify a new book. I therefore thought it might be acceptable if I used a number of the photographs not used in *The Changing Face of Nottingham* and accompanied each of them with one showing what the scene looks like today.

The publishers accepted this idea and this book, *Nottingham Yesterday and Today*, is the result. Taking the new photographs proved an interesting experience. In some cases it was fairly easy to identify where I had stood when I took the earlier photograph. This was usually where there was still some feature that was there in the previous photograph. Others proved rather more of a problem. Although I had indicated on the back of the original photographs where they were taken, it was not always easy to find the place again. This was usually the case where the subsequent new building involved a change in the street pattern. This meant looking up a map of the area before the redevelopment took place and comparing it with a present-day one.

As before, most of the old photographs were taken between about 1955 and 1975. It was from about 1955 that changes in the older part of the city started to take place. There had been little change in the appearance of such parts in the six years from 1939 because new building and demolition of older ones were not allowed because of wartime restrictions. These regulations remained for ten years after the end of the war. New building was confined mainly to the construction of new houses, and in Nottingham these were mostly on land which had not been built on previously. By 1955 the construction of new houses had reached a point where it was possible to start demolishing some of the thousands of older houses which had become worn out and were not capable of being improved. This process was to continue for the next twenty-five years or so. At the same time the opportunity was taken to re-plan the areas of clearance schemes by including other buildings such as factories and workshops, which in the nineteenth century had been built close to the houses where their workers lived. More enlightened town planning involved the separation of industrial zones from residential areas in the redeveloped parts of Nottingham. Many of the older schools were also demolished and replaced by more modern ones.

The growth of motor traffic meant that many of the older streets, especially in the central area, were inadequate, and new street patterns and traffic control systems resulted in changes in the city's appearance. Other modern trends, such as in entertainment and shopping, contributed to changes which have caused Nottingham to be altered in ways which, as in other towns, have meant that people who have not visited the city for some time fail to recognize it. In this book I have tried to find as many examples of these changes as I can. I have not, I hope, allowed my own opinions about whether the changes have been for better or worse to intrude. I leave this to the reader.

The Unitarian Church has moved to other premises on Plumtre Street and its former building is now the Lace Hall. The buildings on Weekday Cross and Drury Hill have all gone to make way for the Broad Marsh Centre and a new road connecting Canal Street with Fletcher Gate.

THE SITE OF THE MEDIEVAL BOROUGH

The photographs in this section are all of places in the historic heart of the city. The earliest map of Nottingham, drawn by John Speed in 1610, showed how small the town was then. Although the borough stretched from Trent Bridge to Mapperley Hills, the only part with buildings was between what is now Canal Street and Upper Parliament Street, with the western boundary being the Castle and the eastern one near the Ice Stadium.

The basic street pattern dates from the earliest Saxon and Norman settlements and the names of some of the streets are known from fourteenth-century documents. These include High Pavement, Lister Gate, Broad Marsh and Hounds Gate, which have all survived, as have others, although the spellings have altered over the centuries.

There are few buildings built before 1700 which have survived, apart from the three churches, because rebuilding started in the eighteenth century. The rapid growth of population and trade in the nineteenth century resulted in more buildings disappearing and being replaced by new ones. The present century has seen this process continuing.

The name of the restaurant is clearly shown. Where was it? (Answer on page 123.)

Long Row and Queen Street. In 1963, Queen's Chambers, designed by Nottingham's exuberant architect, Watson Fothergill, was only sixty-six years old but its brickwork had been discoloured by decades of smoke.

Today, Queen's Chambers has been cleaned to remove the soot, and traffic can no longer travel along Long Row West, as the trees and telephone boxes restrict access.

Poultry/South Parade. The demolition of Farmer's shop and other properties as far as St Peter's Gate in 1974 provided a new view of St Peter's Church for a time.

The new properties built on the cleared site provide a sharp contrast to the unchanged buildings on either side.

Long Row West. One of Nottingham's most popular public houses, Yates's Wine Lodge, is also known as The Talbot. There were two telephone boxes on the pavement, as well as a police box of the kind made famous by Dr Who (partly visible on the right).

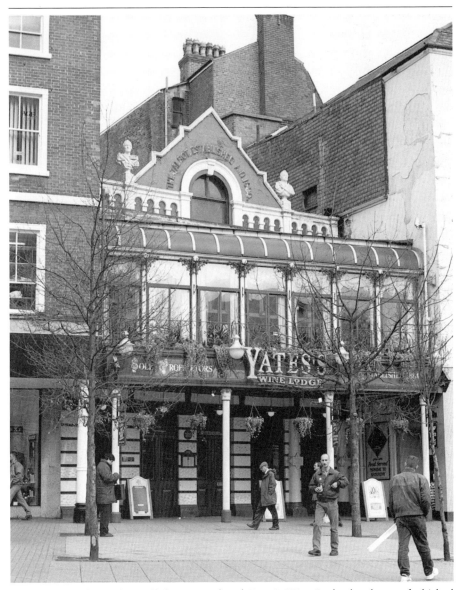

The telephone boxes have all disappeared and Yates's Wine Lodge has been refurbished with a conservatory over the entrance.

Long Row West and Clumber Street. This picture was taken after Skinner & Rook's premises had been demolished and before rebuilding had started. The Lion Hotel is still there.

Clumber Street is now pedestrianized and forms a link between Broad Marsh and Victoria Centre shopping malls. The street furniture now includes the informative direction signpost.

Thurland Street, 1964. The Corn Exchange, erected in 1850, was said to have been designed from a building built by Sir Christopher Wren. It is many years since it was used for its original purpose.

The building which now adjoins the Corn Exchange, now the Clinton Rooms, does not match it, whereas the previous warehouse did.

Lincoln Street, 1962. Clumber Street can be seen on the left, with Clinton Street West on the right. The brick wall concealed the railway line from Victoria station.

The buildings between Clumber Street and Clinton Street West have replaced those in the picture above. The wall on the right is part of premises connected with Victoria Centre by a footbridge.

Thurland Street and Clinton Street. This view of the Council House was opened up in 1964 when Danks' ironmongery shop was demolished. The wall on the right of the picture concealed the railway line from Victoria station which went through the tunnel to Weekday Cross.

Shops with offices above have been erected at the corner of Lincoln Street and Thurland Street, and other new buildings have been built between the two sections of Clinton Street.

Castle Road, 1950s. Taken from near the Castle entrance, the picture shows Walnut Tree Lane and Castle Terrace, with Jessamine Cottage lower down Castle Road.

The People's College buildings now occupy most of the sites cleared of houses and other buildings, including the Colonel Hutchinson public house.

Castle Road. The street to the right is Castle Gate and in 1963 it was a through road to Albert Street. The decorative buildings on Castle Road are further examples of Watson Fothergill's (born Fothergill Watson) designs.

Watson Fothergill's original name has been given to the restaurant which can be seen on the left in the picture, with tables put outside in fine weather. Both Castle Road and the part of Castle Gate as far as Maid Marian Way are now pedestrianized.

Castle Gate. The elegant columns flanking the porch of no. 44 had elaborately carved capitals, believed to have been part of the medieval Lenton Priory.

The columns have disappeared and 44 Castle Gate has now been amalgamated with the adjoining properties to form solicitors' offices.

Castle Gate. The Congregational Church had its own burial ground adjoining the rear of the shops on Albert Street.

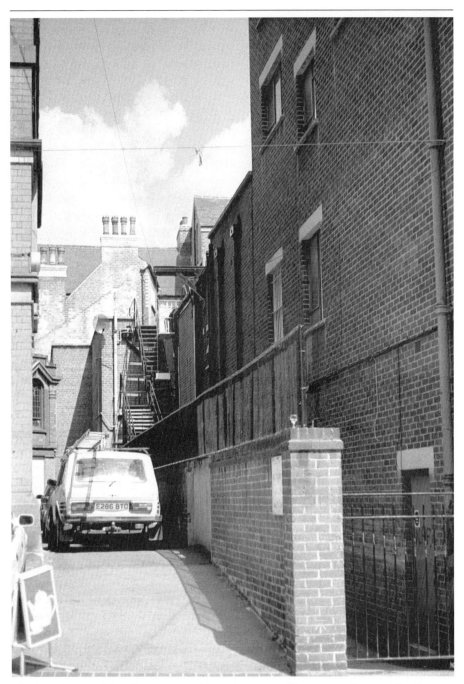

The burial ground has been removed but there are still some tombstones fixed to the wall of the church. The shops on Albert Street have been rebuilt.

Greyfriar Gate. This picture shows Stanford Street from the bottom end looking up to Castle Gate after the buildings had been demolished. The notice board indicates that a well-known store (Woolworth's) was erected on the site.

Greyfriar Gate has disappeared and in this view from the pedestrianized Lister Gate one can just see the buildings on the left-hand side of Stanford Street.

Low Pavement. The former Assembly Rooms were occupied in 1964 by an insurance company and later became a post office for a number of years until recently. The small street on the right next to Marks & Spencer's entrance was Church Gate.

In this picture Church Gate has been replaced by a footway and steps (centre). This may soon disappear as there are proposals to extend Marks & Spencer's premises again.

Church Gate, 1961. This short street connected Low Pavement with St Peter's Church Side and Pepper Street. At the end was a short flight of steps, St Peter's Church Walk to St Peter's Gate. Before Albert Street was made in 1844 Church Gate was part of the main route south from the Market Place.

Marks & Spencer's shop was extended over the site of Church Gate and a narrow walkway and steps form the route to St Peter's Church Walk. Low Pavement has been largely pedestrianized and forms part of a historic trail with information boards.

Spaniel Row. The large building known as Minerva House was only seen like this for a short time after Collin's Almshouses on Friar Lane had been demolished.

City House, seen only on the poster in the picture above, is now a reality at the corner of Friar Lane and Maid Marian Way.

Friar Lane. In 1962 the Friends' Meeting House and Adult School were replaced by a new building on Clarendon Street. The factory to the rear was on St James Street.

In their place is a new block of shops with offices above.

Friar Lane, 1964. The demolition of the adjoining property to provide part of the land for Maid Marian Way left Grosvenor House with a blank wall.

Grosvenor House has been rebuilt in a similar style to its former appearance and a pedestrian subway built at the busy junction of Maid Marian Way and Friar Lane.

St James Street. The lower half runs from Maid Marian Way to the Old Market Square. This photograph was taken in 1964 and a trolley-bus can be seen on Beastmarket Hill.

The scene has not changed radically today but a number of minor differences can be seen, such as the changes of use of the buildings and the changes in the pavements and road surface.

Standard Hill. In 1963 it was still possible to see, at the bottom of Rutland Street, buildings on Granby Street. The one directly facing Rutland Street has gone and Granby Street has been re-named Maid Marian Way.

There is still the open car park in the foreground but the view is now dominated by the multi-storey car park and the tall block, Newtown House.

Park Row, 1968. The Cripples Guild, on the south side of the street, was one of the last buildings to be cleared to complete the extension of Maid Marian Way.

There are now new buildings on both sides of Park Row as well as on the east side of Maid Marian Way, with just a glimpse of the older ones on Upper Parliament Street.

Mortimer Street. Most of the houses and other buildings on this street, Edward Street and Isabella Street were pulled down in the 1930s. In 1955 this view from the cleared site shows the rear of houses on Castle Terrace and Walnut Tree Lane.

The houses were demolished and a considerable amount of levelling took place to allow the People's College to be built, the name being taken from the older premises on The Ropewalk.

Brewhouse Yard. The buildings in this picture, apart from the Trip to Jerusalem inn, were occupied by Nottingham Corporation Water Department.

The eighteenth-century houses have been converted into Brewhouse Yard Museum, with different rooms furnished to show various aspects of Nottingham's earlier history.

Canal Street. In 1964 the cleared site at the junction with Albion Street was used as a temporary surface car park.

The temporary car park has been built on to provide a small covered car park. Albion House, the building on the left of the picture, is new as well, replacing an older building.

Stoney Street, 1965. Taken from the top of Barker Gate, this picture shows the temporary car park on the site of the warehouses which had been demolished to make way for a new street.

The scheme for a new street was abandoned and a car park with offices has been built on the site, in a style to match the adjoining warehouses.

Cliff Road. This quiet street was formerly known as Red Lion Street and Narrow Marsh. It was far from quiet until the 1920s when the former lodging houses and other dwellings were demolished. One building which remained had the painted inscription advertising single and double beds at 3*d* and 6*d* respectively.

The building on which good lodgings were advertised was entered from Cliff Road and extended upwards to commercial premises on Commerce Square. The two were separated by a fireproof floor. The whole building has now been converted into modern flats and the ground floor contains garages. An extra storey has been added.

Pilcher Gate. The building on the right stood at the corner of St Mary's Gate and was probably at one time a large dwelling house. The building on St Mary's Gate was Flersheim's lace warehouse.

The new building on the right is a block of flats extending to Halifax Place, while the car park and offices on St Mary's Gate extends to Stoney Street, the other façade of which can be seen on page 35.

Fletcher Gate and Bottle Lane. The building at the corner of Bottle Lane was originally built as the Sion Chapel in 1819, but had been used for commercial purposes for many years.

The former chapel and the adjoining properties on Fletcher Gate and Bottle Lane have been demolished and the cleared site is awaiting redevelopment.

Pemberton Street. Taken in 1965, this photograph shows the street after most of the buildings had been demolished. It illustrates the way in which the cliff resulted in buildings at different levels.

The building on the cleared site was built as a police station to replace the one at the corner of London Road and Canal Street. It is now used as offices, and the police station has moved again to Station Street.

Fisher Gate, 1971. This picture shows the cleared site, after the houses and shops on the north side had been demolished.

New houses and flats with attractive landscaping have now been built by a housing association.

Woolpack Lane. These dilapidated old houses at the rear of Hockley had survived the reshaping of this part of Nottingham in the 1930s when many former streets disappeared.

The houses were demolished under a clearance order and the site is now used as a car park. Buildings on Lower Parliament Street can be seen today.

Hockley. From Cranbrook Street, seen on the right of the picture, Hockley was the name of the lower part while Goose Gate went up as far as Carlton Street. The names of two former retail shops can be seen.

The road on the left is Belward Street and was constructed as part of the road improvements from London Road.

Lower Parliament Street, 1964. The unusual design of this house, in White Cow Yard, was quite a landmark after adjoining properties had been demolished.

The Ice Stadium car park is in the foreground while just beyond is the Carter Gate Housing Association estate.

Lower Parliament Street, *c.* 1955. The space in front of the Ice Stadium had been a burial ground and when that was closed it had been landscaped as an open space.

The construction of the car park was subject to a condition that some of the trees were replaced.

Hollowstone, 1963. This was formerly the main way into the town until Arkwright Street was made. The Town Arms public house is on the left at the bottom of Malin Hill.

Most of the buildings in this picture have not changed since 1963 but the road has been widened and made into a one-way street, linking up with Bellar Gate and Belward Street.

Lower Parliament Street, 1968. Extending from the end of George Street is Clare Street, a name probably unfamiliar to many people. Before Victoria station was built there were about a hundred houses on Clare Street.

The buildings on either side of Clare Street have not altered a great deal since 1968 but Victoria Centre can now be seen at the end.

Broad Street. The street on the left is Lenton Street, which connects with George Street.

The corner shop and houses on Lenton Street have been demolished and the street widened as part of a one-way system.

Upper Parliament Street, 1962. The building on the left was built as Turkish baths in 1897 but after the Second World War it was used as a clinic. The other building was the Parliament Picture Palace, erected in 1913, and later called the News House and the Odd Hour Cinema.

Both buildings were demolished to provide the site for shops with offices above them.

London Road, 1962. The buildings at the junction with Canal Street were demolished to make way for widening London Road in connection with the traffic control system.

The building erected on the cleared site was a power station for the Boots Company, which was later incorporated into the district heating scheme.

Lower Parliament Street. The buildings in the centre of the picture were on Poplar Street and Plumtre Square. The Roman Catholic Church of Our Lady and St Patrick is the building with a spire on the left.

Most of the buildings have been demolished to form a new one-way street system for traffic to Cranbrook Street.

EARLY EXPANSION AROUND THE TOWN

By 1801, the population of the borough was three times larger than it had been fifty years earlier. The houses to accommodate the increased number of people, together with commercial buildings, took over the sites of gardens and orchards, but when these were used up some expansion took place on the edges of the town.

An important event in the town's development was the opening of the Nottingham Canal in 1796 and this was accompanied by the building of wharves, warehouses and houses near the canal. The railway line from Derby, opened in 1839, was adjacent to the canal and opened up more of the town with the Carrington Street bridge over the canal.

Maps of 1820 and 1831 show that some new building had taken place north of Parliament Street, to the east of Milton Street and along the land between Sherwood Street and Mansfield Road. Further building was not possible until legislation allowed it on the former open fields.

Some of the buildings had already been demolished and the rest went to provide the site for

what? (Answer on page 123.)

Wilford Street. Beyond the railway line were the former bonded stores, which still bore the name of the company, LMS, which ceased to exist when the railways were nationalized.

The view of Nottingham Castle is now partially obscured by the newly erected buildings for the Inland Revenue.

Wilford Street, 1971. The view from the bridge over the Nottingham Canal shows the rear and older portion of Viyella House, which contained offices, warehouses and a factory of William Hollins & Co. Ltd.

Now named New Castle House, the former Hollins building has been largely rebuilt although some of its elegant 1930s features have been retained.

Theatre Square. The County Hotel was built at about the same time as the adjacent Theatre Royal.

The hotel was demolished, along with other properties on Goldsmith Street, to provide a site for the Royal Concert Hall.

Goldsmith Street. The Playhouse, previously known as the Little Theatre and built as a cinema, had closed owing to the opening of the new Playhouse. The Spread Eagle public house next door had taken its name from one opposite which had been demolished.

The old Playhouse has recently been altered to a restaurant, while the public house next door is now called the Goldsmith Pitcher.

Gedling Street. When this picture was taken the building was used as a technical school for the textile trades. It was erected by Nottingham Town Mission in 1859 as a Ragged School.

The original name of the school referred to the dress of the poorest children who attended it, but could now apply to its present state of repair.

Canning Circus. Traffic from Derby Road into the city centre crossed the traffic going outwards, including along Ilkeston Road to the right of the Sir John Borlace Warren public house.

A complete gyratory traffic system of one-way streets goes round Canning Circus now, with the Sir John Borlace Warren and other buildings on an island site.

Ropewalk, 1960s. The large house on the right stands at the junction with Upper College Street and the ornamental garden gives wide views over Nottingham Park. The popular name for this area is the Bay of Biscay.

The garden has changed little but new properties have been built on the north side.

Section Three

THE ENCLOSURE OF THE OPEN FIELDS

The first of the fields north of the town on which development under an Enclosure Act of 1839 was allowed were the Lammas Fields. This was an area north of Park Row, where Wellington Circus and the streets around were laid out and where St Barnabas Roman Catholic Church, later to become a cathedral, was built.

Another small area to be developed about this time was Burton Leys, where Burton Street was laid down and Holy Trinity Church built. The main Enclosure Act of 1845 allowed development on the Sand Field and the Clay Field, to the west and east respectively of Mansfield Road and extending up to Forest Road.

The development of these two fields followed rather different patterns. On the Sand Field large houses were built on Goldsmith Street, Shakespeare Street and the streets north of Shakespeare Street. Large areas were not built on, forming the Central Cemetery and the Arboretum. Later a mixed development of houses and factories was built in the All Saints area. To the east, on the Clay Field, smaller houses were built to form the St Ann's area.

This street was named after which nearby amenity provided for in the Enclosure Act?

(Answer on page 124.)

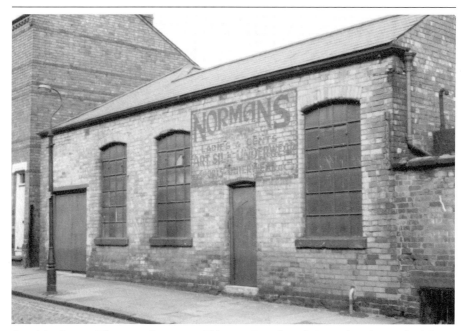

Gamble Street. The area between Alfreton Road and Waverley Street had been developed in the second half of the nineteenth century with houses and factories close together.

The houses which adjoined the small workshop have been demolished, as has part of the workshop itself.

Mansfield Road. Some of the large houses near the junction with Woodborough Road had been adapted for commercial purposes.

All the properties back to Huntingdon Street were demolished and the site used for the erection of a well-designed office block.

Elm Avenue. This tree-lined walk starts at Mansfield Road near the top of Huntingdon Street and stretches up to Corporation Oaks. The section in this picture starts on Cranmer Street.

The elm trees, like so many others throughout the country, suffered from disease and have been replaced.

Ransom Road. The top of the road which started on St Ann's Well Road still had a rural appearance in 1960. The Coppice Hospital can be seen in the distance.

The rural scene has still not entirely disappeared but houses have been built lower down the road.

Robin Hood Chase, 1966. This pleasant tree-lined walk, running from Woodborough Road to St Ann's Well Road, was a planned feature of the development of the former Clay Field.

The southern end, from St Ann's Well Road, has been redeveloped with new houses, shops, a market and library.

Huntingdon Street. By 1975 most of the houses between Huntingdon Street and Alfred Street North had been pulled down, giving views of the factories and workshops on St Ann's Hill Road, as well as the Elms School.

The new houses have been built on a new street pattern but a small section of Alfred Street North with St Andrew's Parish Hall still remains.

Alfred Street North. Originally known as Great Alfred Street, it had a number of terraces, two of which were named after popular heroes of the time, Abraham Lincoln and Guiseppe Garibaldi.

The former crowded streets have given way to walks and closes with more open views.

Great Freeman Street. This picture from 1970 was taken at the junction of Northumberland Street, after clearance was well under way.

The new houses are on Abbotsford Drive, with the tall factory on Ashforth Street providing a reference point.

St Ann's Well Road. In 1968, this busy thoroughfare had houses, shops, cinemas and public houses, the latter including the Westminster Abbey Hotel near the bottom of Ransom Road.

The name is the same, but the public house has been rebuilt near its former site.

Watkin Street, 1966. Shelton Street School can be seen in this picture, taken just off Huntingdon Street.

The school has been demolished and new buildings have been erected on the site. The houses on Watkin Street have not altered very much, but the street itself functions as a car park.

Blue Bell Hill Road, 1972. Taken from just below the old school, this view shows the large factory on Alfred Street South.

The lower half of the Blue Bell Hill Road has been re-named Beacon Hill Rise and new houses have been built on the site of the factory.

Hungerhill Road, 1968. From the top of Westminster Street, St Ann's Valley could be seen on the edge of the built-up area next to the allotment gardens.

The top few yards of Westminster Street still exist, as do the allotment gardens, but new dwellings have been erected along Hungerhill Road and on Broad Oak Close.

St Ann's Valley, 1968. The bay-windowed houses could be seen from Rookwood Road. The stone wall hid one of the few gardens attached to houses in St Ann's.

This view from Broad Oak Close reveals the Hungerhill allotments which backed on to St Ann's Valley.

THE MEADOWS

The Enclosure Act of 1845 also allowed building in The Meadows, the area lying between the canal and the River Trent. These fields, famous for their crocuses in spring, had been wash-lands for the River Trent, as the inhabitants of the houses were to find out in 1932 and 1947 when floods spread as far north as the railway.

A feature of this development was the extension of the roads south from the town, along Carrington Street and then Arkwright Street, to provide an alternative route to Trent Bridge. Streets leading off Arkwright Street contained many narrow terraces of houses, with factories and workshops nearby.

The appearance of The Meadows was altered in the early years of the twentieth century with the building of the Great Central Railway and the construction of Victoria Embankment. Part of The Meadows included land outside the borough boundary, the northern part of Wilford parish. This, together with other parishes, became part of the borough in 1877.

What did the twin towers form part of? (Answer on page 124.)

Wilford Grove. Taken from the end of Ryeland Crescent, the view in 1974, following much demolition, included the remains of the railway line and the depot and chapel on Queen's Drive.

The new houses have the address Ryeland Gardens but the old street nameplate can still be seen on the wall of the end house of the remaining group of Wilford Grove.

Trent Bridge Footway. This footpath was a convenient short cut from Kirkewhite Street to Queen's Road.

The footpath is now called Summer Leys Lane and St Mary's parish marker posts, dated 1852, were until recently to be seen outside the Theatre Royal.

Crocus Street, 1976. The boiler and steel chimney formed a temporary installation to provide district heating until the much larger Eastcroft plant was built.

The houses on Crocus Street were demolished and replaced by industrial buildings with some landscaping. The flowers after which the street was named have not reappeared.

Bunbury Street/Orange Street, 1971. The houses on the left of the large factory were on Kirkby Street and those on the right on Bell Street.

The clearing away of houses and the factory adjoining them has enabled a school with pleasant playgrounds and trees to be built.

London Road. The group of buildings on the left were the Burton Almshouses which were erected in 1859 from a legacy by Miss Ann Burton.

The almshouses were demolished and new ones built in their place elsewhere in The Meadows. A raised grassed bank with trees has been built to minimize traffic noise.

Meadow Lane, 1964. The stone bridge over the Nottingham Canal had revolving iron posts to prevent the ropes by which horses pulled the boats being frayed.

Some of the buildings in the above picture were on Ashling Street and have been demolished. Notts. County FC's new stand can now be seen.

Trent Bridge, 1963. The small garden which adjoined Turney's leather works was at one time the departure point for paddle steamers. The bridge in the distance carried the railway to Melton Mowbray and beyond.

The leather works has now been converted into dwellings and others built adjoining it. The former railway bridge is now a road bridge and the Trent End stand of Nottingham Forest's football ground has been rebuilt.

Trent Bridge, early 1960s. On the south bank was the former Plaza cinema, which at the time of this picture was about to be demolished.

The imposing building on this site was erected as Bridgford Hotel but is now the headquarters of Rushcliffe Borough Council.

Trent Bridge. The Plaza cinema was approached through the white stone porch and then across a footbridge.

A cosmopolitan air is provided by the buildings in front of Rushcliffe Borough Council's headquarters.

SNEINTON

This separate parish, adjacent to the borough on its eastern boundary, took its name from the same Saxon tribal leader as Nottingham itself. It remained a small village until the end of the eighteenth century, when it had a population of only 558. The population increased rapidly in the years after about 1820, more than 400 new houses being erected in the next ten years. This was due mainly to the growth of the bobbin net trade.

Most of the new houses were built near the boundary with Nottingham, this part becoming known as New Sneinton, with another group called Sneinton Elements on Carlton Road. Some of the houses and the streets themselves disappeared a hundred years later, along with neighbouring properties in the city. The City Transport Depot was built on part of the cleared Sneinton site.

The parish was absorbed into the borough in 1877 and in the present century it developed eastwards along Sneinton Dale, Sneinton Boulevard and Colwick Road. Most of the remaining early nineteenth-century properties were demolished in the 1960s.

A building in the distance gives a clue to the location. Which street is it? (Answer on page 125.)

Bentinck Street. Most of the houses had been demolished while those on Kingston Street and in the far centre on Sneinton Road were to go soon afterwards.

The large building seen on both pictures was erected in 1855 as the Albion Congregational Church, but is now used for other purposes.

Manvers Street, 1968. The high wall was part of the London and North Western Railway Company's premises, erected as a goods depot.

The railway site, now hidden by trees, has been used for new houses.

Pennyfoot Street. St Philip's Church was erected in 1879 and the school, shown above, adjoined it. Because of the movement of people away from the district, both were pulled down in 1964.

The cleared site, together with a former playground, has been used for the erection of modern offices.

Windmill Lane. At the east end of Windmill Lane was a small group of houses called Burrows Gardens, approached up the steps in the centre of the picture.

The houses have been pulled down, the area landscaped and the name Burrows given to the multi-storey Court. The Red Cow public house is still there but has lost most of its chimneys.

Lees Hill Street, 1976. The way down to Manvers Street can be seen on the right of this photograph and was known as Lees Hill Footway.

The houses on the footway have been demolished and the sites landscaped. There are extensive views over the Trent Valley from the top of the steps.

Section Six

RADFORD AND LENTON

The development of these two parishes north and west of the old borough followed a similar pattern to that of Sneinton. Again it was the growth of the textile trades in the borough which influenced the growth nearer to the town. Lenton was five times as large as Radford in acreage, but by 1801 the latter already had a population three times as great. Radford grew rapidly in population and by 1831 was the second largest place in Nottinghamshire, being bigger than Mansfield and Newark. Hyson Green was one of the areas of early industrialization and was partly in each of the two parishes. Lenton had a population only half of that of Radford by 1877, when both were taken into the borough.

Many of Radford's older properties were cleared away in the 1930s and later in the 1960s, although much of its street pattern has remained. Lenton, because of its much larger acreage, never became as crowded as Radford and retained much of its rural appearance into the twentieth century.

The row of houses at Radford, on the left of the picture, is still there. To which large firm did

the premises on the right belong? (Answer on page 125.)

Garfield Road, 1977. Opposite Wilton Road this street stretched as far as Denman Street with streets on the left going through to Radford Boulevard.

The street pattern has been radically altered and only a few yards of Garfield Road now remain.

Wilton Road, 1977. This street connected Hartley Road with Beckenham Road. Ellen Terrace is on the right-hand side.

The houses have all been demolished and a new building is being constructed across the line of the street.

Hartley Road. The large building in the foreground was the Nottingham Scattered Home for children in the care of the local authority.

The cleared site has been used for the erection of new dwellings including the multi-storey Broadway Court.

Archer Street, 1960s. This was one of seven streets on the east side of Radford Road, between Gregory Boulevard and Berridge Road. The large building was a Methodist church which later became a boys' club.

All seven streets have disappeared and the area has been redeveloped, first with deck-access flats which only lasted for about twenty years. More traditional houses have now replaced them.

Park Road, Lenton. In 1978 a lace dressing factory situated between Park Road and Castle Boulevard had just been demolished. The chimney which was the last part to go had inscribed on it 'L.W. 1825'.

The cleared site was used for the erection of new warehouses.

Gregory Street. This shows the eastern half of the street between Abbey Street and Lenton Lane, prior to the demolition of the buildings on the south side.

The new houses on the left are called Friary Close. Buildings of the Queen's Medical Centre can be seen in the distance.

Abbey Street, 1971. The three-storey house with a brewhouse next door stood near the junction of Gregory Street.

The cleared site has been fenced off and used as a garden.

Abbey Street. The track on the right of the picture led to Lenton Lane, going under the railway. The site works were for the building of Dunkirk Fire Station.

In place of the track, the Clifton Boulevard flyover crosses over the railway and connects with Clifton Bridge.

University Boulevard. Nottingham University and the City Council share the Highfields site given by Lord Trent, the former Jesse Boot.

The boating lake, overlooked by the pavilion, forms part of University Park with the university occupying the grounds to the rear.

BASFORD AND BULWELL

Basford parish had common boundaries with both Radford and Nottingham. Bulwell to the north of Basford did not have a common boundary with Nottingham. Basford, a large parish, stretched from Cinderhill in the west to Mapperley in the east. Both Basford and Bulwell were on the River Leen which they used for commercial purposes, mainly the bleaching and dyeing of textiles. They both became part of Nottingham in 1877 along with the other adjoining parishes. Their populations had also increased, converting them from small villages to industrial ones because of their proximity to Nottingham.

Basford first expanded early in the nineteenth century with New Basford springing up along the southern boundary with Nottingham. Other settlements were established at about the same time at Carrington and Sherwood on the eastern side alongside the Mansfield Road. Bulwell, with its own industries of quarrying and coal mining, grew more slowly than the other parishes and only reached a population of 5,000 after it was absorbed into the borough. Both Old Basford and Bulwell retained their older appearance together with more modern development until the 1960s.

This small enclosure was formerly the outdoor shopping centre for the village named after a lord.

What was it called? (Answer on page 126.)

Hucknall Road. This section of the road near Birchin Street was widened and the area developed after the Borough of Nottingham was extended in 1877.

The cleared site of the houses has been used as the playing field of a new school.

Mansfield Road, 1962. New Street, Carrington, was probably quite an appropriate name when it was laid down. It is mentioned, as is the New Inn, in a directory of 1853.

The houses on New Street beyond the New Inn were demolished in the 1960s but the inn itself is little changed, apart from the loss of the name of a local brewery.

Southwark Place. This shows the rear of a small group of houses at the ends of Bulwell Lane and Park Lane.

The houses have been demolished and the cleared site has been landscaped giving views of Southwark Street and Rosebery Street.

Bulwell Lane. Before Vernon Road was made, Bulwell Lane was the main route from Basford to Bulwell. The Old Pear Tree public house is mentioned in a directory as early as 1832.

The public house has been refurbished without altering its appearance too much and its name has not been changed, unlike those of many other public houses.

Park Lane. This photograph shows houses at the southern end of the road, near its junction with Arnold Road.

The demolition of the old houses has enabled the road to be widened, and buses now travel along it.

Park Lane. This shows the northern end of the road, near its junction with Brooklyn Road.

The grassed area and trees form a barrier against traffic noise for the occupants of the new houses on Stoneycroft Road.

Arnold Road. This picture, taken from near the end of Edwards Lane, shows some of the last remaining farmland in the city in the 1950s.

The Bestwood Park estate was built in stages and a new road, Beckhampton Road, leads into it.

Duke Street, 1962. The builders of these houses, rather more elegant than the terraced houses nearby, were sufficiently proud of them to put a date stone, 1852, in the pediment.

Most of the houses in this street, as well as others in the area, when demolished, were replaced by light industrial buildings.

Nuthall Road. The nurseries were almost opposite Llanberis Grove and the pre-decimalization prices seem quite a bargain.

The site has been developed by the erection of a small housing scheme, around Keverne Close.

Ravensworth Road. This group of three houses, known as Ravensworth Villas, was near Stockton Street. The houses were rather more stylish than most of the nineteenth-century houses in Bulwell.

The cleared site has been used for the new Methodist Church.

Stone Row. This small row of houses was at the bottom of Chatham Street, close to the footbridge over the railway line.

The new houses in the redeveloped Highbury Vale area have a different street pattern but the names of former streets have been retained.

Section Eight

EXPANSION IN THE TWENTIETH CENTURY

The borough as extended in 1877 continued to grow in population and with the development of new buildings until the 1930s. The creation of new council housing estates after 1919 started to use up undeveloped land, mainly fields and agricultural land on the edges of the city. Some of these then extended over the county border and in the 1930s parts of Bestwood, Bilborough, Colwick and Wollaton were also absorbed into the city. There were few existing properties in these areas and so their appearance is relatively recent.

After the end of the Second World War, further land for council housing was needed south of the city, and the village of Clifton with most of its farmland undeveloped was acquired. The large Clifton estate was built mainly to the east away from the village. Clifton became part of the city in 1952, together with the village of Wilford lying south of the River Trent.

A directory of 1832 refers to 'several neat villas belonging to opulent families engaged in the trade and commerce of Nottingham'. What was the name of this house? (Answer on page 126.)

Wilford. The toll bridge, known to foot passengers as the ha'penny bridge, was built to replace a ferry in 1870. Clifton Colliery seen on the river bank was sunk at the same time.

The toll bridge has been replaced by a new structure for pedestrians and cyclists only, and the colliery by an industrial and trading estate.

Victoria Embankment. The bridge in the foreground was the one that carried the railway line over the River Trent. The reconstructed toll bridge is a little way upstream.

The railway bridge has been demolished as the line from Victoria station to Marylebone has been taken up.

Wilford, 1964. The approach to the crossroads at Wilford Green had a sign warning of the junction with Main Road.

Today traffic lights control the flow along the road, which has been widened on its north side.

Wilford Green. Wilford House, an eighteenth-century house built for the Smiths, Nottingham's pioneer bankers, was largely hidden by trees in 1964.

The increase in traffic has meant the installation of traffic lights and guard-rails. Wilford House has been renovated and extended in an attractive style.

Wilford. The electricity generating station was built in 1926 and extended in the late 1940s. It became part of the National Grid and used coal as its fuel. The Clifton Colliery seen on the right was next door.

Both the colliery and the generating station have completely disappeared, apart from the electricity pylons. The sites now have a variety of buildings on them, both retail and manufacturing.

Clifton. The hump-backed bridge over the Fairham Brook formed part of the approach to Clifton Grove.

When the new Clifton Bridge over the River Trent was built, the bridge over the Fairham Brook disappeared and a more modern one was built in its place.

Glapton. The road from Ruddington to Clifton ended opposite Clifton Green, the parish's name being Clifton-cum-Glapton.

Glapton Lane is now part of the housing estate, and traffic lights and a pedestrian crossing provide an entrance to Clifton village.

Glapton. There were only a few houses in Glapton and this one was demolished although part of its construction, a cruck, was preserved.

These new houses have been built, but there is still an older house with a date stone of 1879 just opposite them.

Clifton. Before 1950, when work on the large housing estate began, Clifton was still a small rural village.

The village itself has remained largely unchanged, despite its proximity to the housing estate and Nottingham Trent University. It is designated as a conservation area.

Section One, page 7. The building, Severn's, was on Middle Pavement but has been rebuilt on Castle Road. Middle Pavement now has an entrance to Broad Marsh Centre.

Section Two, page 53. This was East Circus Street in 1960 after the Hall had been demolished to make way for Nottingham Playhouse.

Section Three, page 61. The elegant houses on Arboretum Street were typical of those built on the Sand Field. This group was demolished to provide more accommodation for Nottingham High School for Girls.

Section Four, page 75. The remains of Arkwright Street railway station were still visible for a time after the line had been removed. A small section of Arkwright Street can still be seen today.

Section Five, page 85. Shops and trolley-bus wires were much in evidence in Manvers Street and the tower of Victoria Baths, seen in the distance, is still there.

Section Six, page 91. The Player's factories which dominated the scene of Radford churchyard have disappeared and part of the churchyard has been landscaped as a public park.

Section Seven, page 101. Carrington Market Place had long since ceased to be used as such and the site was grassed over. Wesley Street today has a street sign which tells us that it was formerly Carrington Market Place.

Section Eight, page 113. The house was called Wilford Grange and its site was used for a small estate, Grange Close.

BRITAIN IN OLD PHOTOGRAPHS

To order any of these titles please telephone Littlehampton Book Services on 01903 721596

Scunthorpe, *D Taylor*
Skegness, *W Kime*
Around Skegness, *W Kime*

LONDON

Balham and Tooting, *P Loobey*
Crystal Palace, Penge & Anerley, *M Scott*
Greenwich and Woolwich, *K Clark*
Hackney: A Second Selection, *D Mander*
Lewisham and Deptford, *J Coulter*
Lewisham and Deptford: A Second Selection, *J Coulter*
Streatham, *P Loobey*
Around Whetstone and North Finchley, *J Heathfield*
Woolwich, *B Evans*

MONMOUTHSHIRE

Chepstow and the River Wye, *A Rainsbury*
Monmouth and the River Wye, *Monmouth Museum*

NORFOLK

Great Yarmouth, *M Teun*
Norwich, *M Colman*
Wymondham and Attleborough, *P Yaxley*

NORTHAMPTONSHIRE

Around Stony Stratford, *A Lambert*

NOTTINGHAMSHIRE

Arnold and Bestwood, *M Spick*
Arnold and Bestwood: A Second Selection, *M Spick*
Changing Face of Nottingham, *G Oldfield*
Mansfield, *Old Mansfield Society*
Around Newark, *T Warner*
Nottingham: 1944–1974, *D Whitworth*
Sherwood Forest, *D Ottewell*
Victorian Nottingham, *M Payne*

OXFORDSHIRE

Around Abingdon, *P Horn*
Banburyshire, *M Barnett & S Gosling*
Burford, *A Jewell*
Around Didcot and the Hagbournes, *B Lingham*
Garsington, *M Gunther*
Around Henley-on-Thames, *S Ellis*
Oxford: The University, *J Rhodes*
Thame to Watlington, *N Hood*
Around Wallingford, *D Beasley*
Witney, *T Worley*
Around Witney, *C Mitchell*
Witney District, *T Worley*
Around Woodstock, *J Bond*

POWYS

Brecon, *Brecknock Museum*
Welshpool, *E Bredsdorff*

SHROPSHIRE

Shrewsbury, *D Trumper*
Whitchurch to Market Drayton, *M Morris*

SOMERSET

Bath, *J Hudson*
Bridgwater and the River Parrett, *R Fitzhugh*
Bristol, *D Moorcroft & N Campbell-Sharp*
Changing Face of Keynsham,
  B Lowe & M Whitehead

Chard and Ilminster, *G Gosling & F Huddy*
Crewkerne and the Ham Stone Villages,
  G Gosling & F Huddy
Around Keynsham and Saltford, *B Lowe & T Brown*
Midsomer Norton and Radstock, *C Howell*
Somerton, Ilchester and Langport, *G Gosling & F Huddy*
Taunton, *N Chipchase*
Around Taunton, *N Chipchase*
Wells, *C Howell*
Weston-Super-Mare, *S Poole*
Around Weston-Super-Mare, *S Poole*
West Somerset Villages, *K Houghton & L Thomas*

STAFFORDSHIRE

Aldridge, *J Farrow*
Bilston, *E Rees*
Black Country Transport: Aviation, *A Brew*
Around Burton upon Trent, *G Sowerby & R Farman*
Bushbury, *A Chatwin, M Mills & E Rees*
Around Cannock, *M Mills & S Belcher*
Around Leek, *R Poole*
Lichfield, *H Clayton & K Simmons*
Around Pattingham and Wombourne, *M Griffiths,*
  P Leigh & M Mills
Around Rugeley, *T Randall & J Anslow*
Smethwick, *J Maddison*
Stafford, *J Anslow & T Randall*
Around Stafford, *J Anslow & T Randall*
Stoke-on-Trent, *I Lawley*
Around Tamworth, *R Sulima*
Around Tettenhall and Codsall, *M Mills*
Tipton, Wednesbury and Darlaston, *R Pearson*
Walsall, *D Gilbert & M Lewis*
Wednesbury, *I Bott*
West Bromwich, *R Pearson*

SUFFOLK

Ipswich: A Second Selection, *D Kindred*
Around Ipswich, *D Kindred*
Around Mildenhall, *C Dring*
Southwold to Aldeburgh, *H Phelps*
Around Woodbridge, *H Phelps*

SURREY

Cheam and Belmont, *P Berry*
Croydon, *S Bligh*
Dorking and District, *K Harding*
Around Dorking, *A Jackson*
Around Epsom, *P Berry*
Farnham: A Second Selection, *J Parratt*
Around Haslemere and Hindhead, *T Winter & G Collyer*
Richmond, *Richmond Local History Society*
Sutton, *P Berry*

SUSSEX

Arundel and the Arun Valley, *J Godfrey*
Bishopstone and Seaford, *P Pople & P Berry*
Brighton and Hove, *J Middleton*
Brighton and Hove: A Second Selection, *J Middleton*
Around Crawley, *M Goldsmith*
Hastings, *P Haines*
Hastings: A Second Selection, *P Haines*
Around Haywards Heath, *J Middleton*
Around Heathfield, *A Gillet & B Russell*
Around Heathfield: A Second Selection,
  A Gillet & B Russell
High Weald, *B Harwood*
High Weald: A Second Selection, *B Harwood*
Horsham and District, *T Wales*

Lewes, *J Middleton*
RAF Tangmere, *A Saunders*
Around Rye, *A Dickinson*
Around Worthing, *S White*

WARWICKSHIRE

Along the Avon from Stratford to Tewkesbury, *J Jeremiah*
Bedworth, *J Burton*
Coventry, *D McGrory*
Around Coventry, *D McGrory*
Nuneaton, *S Clews & S Vaughan*
Around Royal Leamington Spa, *J Cameron*
Around Royal Leamington Spa: A Second Selection,
  J Cameron
Around Warwick, *R Booth*

WESTMORLAND

Eden Valley, *J Marsh*
Kendal, *M & P Duff*
South Westmorland Villages, *J Marsh*
Westmorland Lakes, *J Marsh*

WILTSHIRE

Around Amesbury, *P Daniels*
Chippenham and Lacock, *A Wilson & M Wilson*
Around Corsham and Box, *A Wilson & M Wilson*
Around Devizes, *D Buxton*
Around Highworth, *G Tanner*
Around Highworth and Faringdon, *G Tanner*
Around Malmesbury, *A Wilson*
Marlborough: A Second Selection, *P Colman*
Around Melksham,
  Melksham and District Historical Association
Nadder Valley, *R. Sawyer*
Salisbury, *P Saunders*
Salisbury: A Second Selection, *P Daniels*
Salisbury: A Third Selection, *P Daniels*
Around Salisbury, *P Daniels*
Swindon: A Third Selection, *The Swindon Society*
Swindon: A Fourth Selection, *The Swindon Society*
Trowbridge, *M Marshman*
Around Wilton, *P Daniels*
Around Wootton Bassett, Cricklade and Purton, *T Sharp*

WORCESTERSHIRE

Evesham to Bredon, *F Archer*
Around Malvern, *K Smith*
Around Pershore, *M Dowty*
Redditch and the Needle District, *R Saunders*
Redditch: A Second Selection, *R Saunders*
Around Tenbury Wells, *D Green*
Worcester, *M Dowty*
Around Worcester, *R Jones*
Worcester in a Day, *M Dowty*
Worcestershire at Work, *R Jones*

YORKSHIRE

Huddersfield: A Second Selection, *H Wheeler*
Huddersfield: A Third Selection, *H Wheeler*
Leeds Road and Rail, *R Vickers*
Pontefract, *R van Riel*
Scarborough, *D Coggins*
Scarborough's War Years, *R Percy*
Skipton and the Dales, *Friends of the Craven Museum*
Around Skipton-in-Craven, *Friends of the Craven Museum*
Yorkshire Wolds, *I & M Sumner*